Sid-ca...

Written by Jan Burchett and Sara Vogler
Illustrated by Jess Mikhail

I am Sid.

This is my Sid-cam.

Join me in the garden.
It is dark.

But I can turn on my torch.
Now we can see.

Let's look for things in the garden.

Can you see the lights?

Wow! It is a star ship from Mars!

Look, they will not hurt me!

Can you see that thing lurking in the garden? Wow! It is a yowling thing from Mars.

Look, it will not hurt me!

Can you see the big, prowling thing?

The big, prowling thing with
the fin ...

13

Look, the big, prowling thing is pointing at me!

Run! It is a Nan shark from Mars!